BREAD AND STONES

Genesis of a Soul

ANNE MORRELL

Lisnalarach Press

First Edition published 2016
Lisnalarach Press

www.breadandstones.com

Typeset and Cover layout by 2QT Limited (Publishing)

Printed in Great Britain
CMP (UK) Limited

A CIP catalogue record for this book is available
from the British Library
ISBN 978-0-9935793-0-1

Preface

Bread and Stones is a moving document. It is a courageous encounter with terrible loss and acute anguish, which are faced, endured and worked through rather than repressed, denied or allowed to dominate. It points towards integration and a future transcendence which cannot be equated with happiness - happiness is not the point - but which can suggest a profundity of being which would be unattainable without the encounter with darkness that preceded it. This story of psychological suffering, endurance and growth is written with quiet eloquence and restraint. It is the account of a journey which many of us, in our own individual ways, make, as did Dante.

E quindi uscimmo a riveder le stelle
(and thence we came forth again to see the stars)

Charlotte Graves Taylor ix 2015

Acknowledgements

Bread and Stones began as a cathartic outpouring of emotional and spiritual anguish following the events of 1997/8. I am very grateful for those friends who connected with me during some, if not all, of those dark and difficult years. In particular, special thanks to Elizabeth Hole and Roberta Irving, Ann and Russ Rusby, Margaret Silf, Peter Kenney and Terry Hurst.

Bread and Stones emerged in this final form during the months following my retirement in 2013. I am immensely grateful to Margaret Silf, Max Gillespie and Charlotte Graves Taylor who, as friends and writers, were willing to read the raw drafts. Their response encouraged me towards its conclusion.

I owe a huge debt to my artist friend and neighbour, Jill York, whose patient tuition enabled me to gain sufficient skill to produce the illustrations. There were many days when I felt I had set myself too hard a challenge but Jill's support and encouragement never faltered. It has been great fun to work with her on this project.

My deep appreciation is extended to Dave Mitchell for the sound recording on the audio version of this work. His understanding of and sensitivity towards the text, alongside his technical expertise, made the whole experience both rich and rewarding. It has been a joy to work with him on this project.

For all that is, all that has been,
and all that will be,
I dedicate this to my dearly loved son,
Chris

Contents

Section One: Bread and Stones

Here Is a Hard Place   11
Here Is a Marriage   15
Here Is a Place of Rejection   19
Here Is a Place of Loss   23
Here Is a Place of Disorientation   27
Here Is a Place of Destruction   31
Here Is a Place of Severance   35

Section Two: Seeds and Pebbles

Here Is a Place of Return   41
Here Is a Child   45
Here Is a Family   49
Here Is a Student   53
Here Is Barrenness   57
Here Is Adoption   61

Section Three: Stones and Bread

Here Is a Place of Desolation   67
Here Is a Place both Familiar and Strange   71
Here Is a Place of Searching   75
Here Is a Place of Meandering   79
Here Everything Is Whole, Nothing is Complete 83
Here Everything Is both Lost and Found   87
Here Is a Place of Emergence   91

Section One
Bread and Stones

'What man is there of you,
who if his son asks for bread
will give him a stone?'
Matthew 7:9

Here

Is a Place of Severance

'TWO shall become one'
Now one has to become two

This wound feels mortal
The mind fragments
A thousand shattered pieces
cracking, collapsing

Fear spills out of the smashed
corridors of thought
Raging images bombard
the shadows, memories
of things said, done
undone, taunting, mocking
Distorting the echoes
of my footfall
Impossible to outrun

A pile of rubble
Beyond repair
My pen is dry

Section Two

Seeds and Pebbles

Here

Is a Place of Return

FROM the other side
of the bridge
I become aware
of you, shrouded
in stillness
Waiting, watching

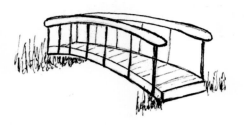

Compelled
I turn to face you
my almost-adult self
Fear choking your desire
veiling the hope
that longs
for an awakening kiss

DARE I come to you?
Cross the span
of the years, wearied
with wasted passion
broken hopes
scattered dreams

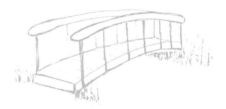

Only by coming
can I gather the seeds
of my recovery

Here

Is a Child

BIBLE classes and scripture
exams passed with top marks
Legs, twisted round podium chairs
too short to reach the floor, awaiting
the embarrassing moment of public
acclaim for success. Dressed
by mother for whom it was really
important that I looked the part
Did I look nice?

Creeping into the spare bed
in my youngest sister's room
ashamed and embarrassed
afraid of sleeping alone
in the dark, night shadows
from the lamp-lighted trees
coming to life in dreams

Disturbed by intense feelings
arriving unannounced, unwelcome
visitors hurrying the heart, swallowed
but not digested. Buried deep
with colossal shovels of will
restless tormentors
unrecognised allies
seldom still

PETRIFIED of the teachers, never
doing anything wrong but always
expecting to be in trouble and yet
when asked, narrating the school
Christmas play, aged five, before
a huge audience. Hiding at the back
of the class, head down, willing
myself out of sight, never answering
a question, breathing silent
desperate prayers for help and yet
aged thirteen, responding to a
teacher's challenge proposing
the motion for the existence of God
in a school debate and winning

Attending a production
of *The Merchant Of Venice* at Stratford
Holding my breath as Portia's almost
whispered dilemma of choice changed
the audience air, spiking dormant hairs
at the back of the neck
Suspended in palpable silence
dissolving the veil separating the here
and now from the beyond and forever

Revising for exams accompanied by
Beethoven's symphonies stacked
on a gramophone, dropping one by one
discharging poetry in sound, matching
cadence to memory

Here

Is a Family

GRACE before meals
Chapel twice on Sundays
Dad was an only child of older
parents, he was a Methodist
preacher, a good one. His was
a lived-in, lived-out faith

Mum was one of seven
in a matriarchal Methodist
family, their invading
presence a curate's egg
Uneasy suspense pervaded
connection, religious
respectability the conforming
melody

Communication was never
clear and straightforward
Nuance of mood orchestrated
behaviour. Conditioned
to respond to its dissonant
theme, I never achieved
the faultless performance
required

TENSION trundled interminably
along underground tracks
Multiple rhythms at odds
with outward appearances
Sifting substance from semblance
a perpetual struggle

Unable to deny a nagging
persistent, ill-at-easeness
I spoke of what I felt, unaware
that it would derail the system

The family collided, confused
Each of us, bruised, battered
bewildered. As we staggered
back on track it dawned on me
that I had been uncoupled

Here

Is a Student

INSPIRED by the teacher
who stepped into my fear-bound
prison, encouraging tentative steps
over the threshold, I decided
to train to teach

I selected a college with a religious
foundation, hoping a known
framework might mitigate
the unknown

Exam results were sufficient
for university. It never occurred
to me that I was good enough
to go

Learning and study called
from a distance, never
absorbing their deserved
attention. Too much energy
needed to overcome a thick
lump of homesickness
hindering the swallowing
of food

CRIPPLING shyness inhibited
friendship, debilitating self-doubt
hounded all pursuits

George Eliot whispered possibilities
of understanding and becoming
TS Eliot nudged towards an embrace
of the almost imperceptible, rustlings
ignored in the zeal of renewed religious
experience but eternally present
in the spirit's shadowed hinterland

The emerging rosebud
of sexual promise
Plucked
before it had time
to bloom
Taken, not given

Pale, delicate petals
bruised and crushed
Forever doubting
their own beauty

Here

Is Barrenness

I WAS a farmer's daughter, geld
cows were sent for slaughter

Investigations complete
summoned to a consulting room
told to undress. An unknown doctor
appeared, dreaded words delivered
devoid of compassion
'You'll never conceive your own child'

Why the indignity
of unnecessary déshabillé?

Outside, the world looked
exactly the same, the sun
still shone, clothing
the trees in brilliant gold
Buses throatily engaged gear
Children crunched leaves
running, laughing
Didn't they know?
My world had changed
For ever

STAMPED 'defective'
Loss of all that had been longed for,
all that now could never be
Grief misunderstood
On my own with a broken heart

Let not this cup
pass from me
Drinking its bitterness
to the last drop

Walking the edge
between sea and shore
spitting rain, salty tears
sympathetic sea spray

A silent, suffering
departed presence
sufficient grace

Here

Is Adoption

THE long awaited phone call
comes, erasing, in an instant
months of ordeal, interviews
reports, panel decisions
A baby needs a home

The foster mother hands me
a bundle and a bottle
A tiny face looks out cradled
in the crook of my arm
Delight and relief dissolve
self-consciousness. I hold him close
and smooth his worried brow
'Hello, little one, welcome home'

More accustomed to the cold
of disappointment and sorrow
it takes some time to get used
to the radiating warmth
of happiness

Not flesh of my flesh, origins
largely unknown, his personality
explodes into my world

BRIMMING with energy and full
of fun, he challenges every boundary
A roller coaster ride of risk
and reward, a daily balancing act
between freedom and constraint

His nonconformity is unappreciated
at school, casting a shadow
over his sunshine world

I record the story of his adoption
in a little book with photographs
We read it together so that
he grows up knowing
his Anglo-Asian heritage
is something to be proud of
The door always open
for him to find out more

The start of a lifetime's relationship
of love, learning each other's
language, holding on through
the despair, the frustrations
and the tears, the stuff
of motherhood

Section Three
Stones and Bread

*'The finest workers in stone are not copper
or steel tools but the gentle touch
of air and water together working
at their leisure with a liberal
allowance of time'*
Henry David Thoreau

Here

Is a Place of Desolation

I SEEK the God
who had always been
with me. He isn't there
Deep shadows ring my eyes
If I speak my pain
is not relieved
If I refrain from speaking
I am not consoled

I hope for peace
Torment comes
I look for light
Darkness comes
I work harder and harder
at spiritual practice
failing spectacularly

Devotion and service to God
had been my lifeblood
quickening the energy
to counter personal frailty
finding expression in ministry
marriage and motherhood

NOW, the words of the liturgy
are as granite, empty
of nourishment
impossible to digest

How do you find
meaning in emptiness?

The thread left hanging
swings frayed
at the mercy
of the elements
The heart searches
for a steadying truth

Does my very longing
alienate that which it seeks?

The wind blows where it wills
Mystery needs time and space
to reveal itself
Or not

Here

Is a Place both
Familiar and Strange

THE service in church
follows its oft-repeated
pattern. Long-remembered
hymns, prayers, readings
sweep up the worship
of the gathered, nourishing
restoring, energising

Not for me

This is an alien
homecoming. I am
a stranger in my own land
These well-worn shoes
are full of holes

THE guttering candle
dances
a different tune
Trembling with each
invisible breath
of air

Alive with light
animating the stones
softening
the shadows

My flame
burns low
Is it enough?

Here

Is a Place of Searching

NEEDING to recover
lost meaning I retreat
to a place of sanctuary
Inside, the stones
of the building
breathe a still
and silent welcome

Four days alone
in the fear-riven
corridors of my mind

Hunched
Swaddled
in layers of clothes
Scalding tears
burning spattered
flesh

I sit
at the window
Gazing at the tree
which stands
spiked
and barren

FRAGMENTING
the weakened
sunlight
Pale yellow droplets
sparkling
on a dew-laden lawn

No sense
of time or space
No coherent thought

Only emptiness
in the aching silence

No revelation

Later, the diamonds
fashioned by sun
and rain return to mind
Gifts, half understood
elusive, half remembered
Sparkling

Here

Everything is Whole, Nothing is Complete

I WENT on a pilgrimage
and discovered that my life
is already a pilgrimage

Gossamer threads of arrivals
and endings weaving
their own unique design

Nothing is finished
Everything is fulfilled

Restoration is imbued
with brokenness
Discord leaps
in and out of harmony

The light plays with its shadow
Revealing and concealing
the hiddenness of things

FEAR nibbles the coat tails
of freedom
A soul's strength
is fashioned in weakness

The wood carved
with the grain
The wood scarred
against the grain
Each displays its image

The pain of engagement
The barrenness
of disengagement
Each has its price

Refusing to deny
woundedness
Refusing to defend
against it, holding
its unbearable reality

Opening up the space
where life is lived
A creative offering
born of waiting

Here

Everything is both

Lost and Found

DISLODGED from the family
Expelled from the marriage
Displaced from the church

No point of return
No crew, no captain
Only the endless horizon

All is movement now
beyond, behind, beneath
safety swallowed in ceaseless
ebb and flow

I am a landlubber
How do I live in the ocean?
Learning not to panic
when the breakers
overwhelm, surfacing
in due time, to live again

Daring to ride the current
as it changes and disappears
awaiting its reappearance
in a fresh place. Each new surge
uncompromising and demanding

LOOKING at the shoreline
knowing I would
have preferred the stability
of the land-locked, framed
in the continuity
of family and faith

The strand
where stones
of all shapes and sizes
claim land against
the rhythm of the tide

The deep
where stones
of all shapes and sizes
are swallowed and fashioned

This is a space
where words are silenced
Longings, hopes, fears
and loves tossed
into the vastness
Where the only thing known
is that nothing is known
Brief glances from an endlessly
elusive mystery

Here

Is a Place of Emergence

WHERE winter's dust
is disturbed, floating
fragments weave the air
threading the sunlight
The dawning of a new
sense, shifting the flow
of energy, changing
the colour of the mind

Ushering in the courage
to pretend less
to our inner selves
To face the fear and refuse
its imprisonment, to seek
that which builds and shun
that which destroys

Illuminating the sight
To recognise
the transfigured ordinary
To participate in its becoming
To value the privilege

Ennobling the heart to reach
beyond its self-absorbed needs
To play a bigger part, to absorb
wickedness eschewing bitterness

FUELLING the anger to take
action against injustice
cruelty, want or neglect
To refuse to be bound
by desire or dread
To fight for the good of all

Releasing the oil of compassion
To recognise our neighbour's need
To bear each other's burdens
To know how to care
and bring comfort

Where winter's dust
is disturbed, floating
fragments weave the air
threading the sunlight
The dawning of a new
sense, shifting the flow
of energy, changing
the colour of the mind